❖

Santa's Take on Parenting

Secrets from the North Pole

❖

Cover design by Jeremiah Trujillo. The Santa and Mrs. Claus image is from a 1919 postcard in the public domain. The story behind its selection is as follows. The Clauses would not allow me to take any photos. Originally our plan was to have a glass of milk and a plate of cookies or perhaps a candy cane on the cover. But one evening around 11:30, as I came down the dark stairs to go to the kitchen for a snack, I saw Santa and Mrs. Claus sitting on the sofa in front of the fire. Mrs. Claus was leaning her head on Santa's shoulder. They were happily looking at old photos one by one. The next morning Mrs. Claus showed me an old postcard they had rediscovered the night before. "We are very fond of it." she said. "In fact, we would like you to use it on the book cover. I like it because it brings back special memories of that time in our lives. Santa likes it because he didn't have to wear glasses back then!"

Santa's Take on Parenting

❖

Secrets from the North Pole

Roland Trujillo

This book is dedicated to children everywhere.

"I love these little people; and it is not a slight thing,
when they, who are so fresh from God, love us."
Charles Dickens

CONTENTS

Introduction

You can imagine my surprise when I began to notice hits on my website coming from the North Pole. A few days later I received an order for my parenting e-book from someone named S. Claus.

Frankly it was only in retrospect that I put two and two together. The obvious conclusion—that Santa Claus had visited my website and had ordered one of my books—was too fanciful to even think of at the time.

A few weeks went by and then one spring morning in early May around 10:00 AM, I received the phone call that would change my life.

I was sitting at the computer when the phone rang. I finished the sentence I was typing and then answered with the usual "Roland speaking."

There was a delay on the other end (which I later learned had to do with the distance and phone services involved), and then a booming, deep voice announced:

"Roland, this is Santa Claus. I wish to discuss a project with you."

Whether it was the hits from the North Pole on my website, the book order from S. Claus, or the warm sincere sound of the voice at the other end, I do not know—but somehow I immediately knew that it was him and no one else.

As if we were old friends, he dispensed with formalities and got down to business right away.

Santa quickly briefed me on the reason for his call. For a long time he had wanted to reach out to parents about some issues he felt strongly about. He searched the Internet for someone who had a concern for children and whose philosophy was, as he phrased it, "compatible" with his. He announced that he had "selected me."

"Selected me for what, Sir?" I asked without a clue.

"I want you to visit Mrs. Claus and me at the North Pole for the purpose of getting my take on some parenting issues for the book I want you to write," Santa said flatly as if it were a foregone conclusion.

I was so surprised by what I had just heard that I stammered and didn't know what to say. Finally I got my act together and said, "Obviously, I'm very flattered, but I must politely and respectfully decline."

I went on to give him many logical reasons (and if memory serves me correctly, many illogical ones) why he should find someone else: someone with a big following, someone with more books to their credit, someone younger, someone older, or someone with friends in high places.

When I was done, Santa, who had been listening patiently, said, "no need to say 'sir.' Just call me Santa."

I think I gave him some more reasons to find someone else, but my words were met with the same silence, then: "Would June work for you or is July better?" Looking back on the conversation, I am now embarrassed at how much of Santa's time I took up.

I was like a kid giving the gym coach all the logical excuses in the world why he (the kid) couldn't do the cartwheel the coach was asking him to do. The kid would argue he's not big enough, not old enough, not feeling well, not ready yet etc. etc. But coach made him do one anyway. Later the child would excitedly tell his mom that he had done his first cartwheel in tumbling class. It was a thrilling accomplishment--one that never would have happened if the coach had listened to all of his "valid, logical" excuses.

I was like that kid, telling Santa why I couldn't do the interview or write the book. By ignoring all my protestations, he was patiently but firmly saying: "You can do it."

I'm glad he didn't listen to me.

Well, so much for that. Now I guess I'd better fill you in on a few preliminary details before we delve into the subject matter.

I know some of you are going to ask just exactly where Santa is located. Sorry, I can't tell you.

I had to sign a non-disclosure agreement to not divulge Santa's location. I readily agreed, but frankly the logistics involved in getting there are so complicated that I couldn't tell you his location even if I wanted to.

I will say that everything was otherwise very informal, with one exception. My luggage was thoroughly scanned and I had to take everything out of my pockets for a security person who (I later learned) was making sure that I did not have a camera, cell phone, or GPS device with me.

The interview took place mostly in person. I was invited to the Claus residence near the North Pole for two separate visits, two months apart. Each visit lasted four days. There were also many phone calls and email exchanges during the process of putting the book together.

I would also like to mention Kylie and Jonathan, two delightful children who you will soon meet in the book. Kylie and Jonathan had actually stayed with the Clauses for a few months a couple of years before my brief visits.

The Clauses were very fond of Jonathan and Kylie and frequently mentioned them. I interviewed Jonathan, Kylie and their mom by phone as part of the book project.

Then, as luck would have it, the Clauses invited Kylie and Jonathan to revisit them at the time of my second visit. It was a great pleasure to meet them in person. I know you will like them too.

I am not allowed to state the dates of my visits or even the year, but I am allowed to say that my visits were during the summer. Fall and early winter are too hectic at the North Pole to leave much time for anything else. After Christmas things do quiet down, but the weather is a bit formidable for someone who is not used to it, and travel can be kind of iffy. So summer was the obvious choice.

The trips up and back went very well (Mrs. Claus did a wonderful job planning the itinerary, and she had one of her assistants make all the reservations).

I have to tell you that I knew I was going to be in for a great experience from the moment I first met Santa in person.

My trip up consisted of commercial jet, then charter jet, then single engine ski plane, a half hour overland trip by 4-wheel-drive to a helicopter pad where one was ready and warmed up to fly me northwest to a clearing near a glacier. From there I traveled by dogsled.

The dogsled driver left me cold and shivering at a small outpost staffed by two nice gentlemen who were doing some sort of weather research. They knew I was coming, as Mrs. Claus had radioed them to expect me.

They were very cordial, inviting me in to sit by the stove and warm up while I waited for Santa. I could smell some hot coffee brewing.

We were sitting at the small dining table talking about the economy when all of a sudden there was a noise outside that I can hardly describe. It was a tremendous whoosh sound, together with the sound of many small bells, and a then deep voice saying something.

"Santa's sleigh's arriving," they said matter-of-factly.

We put on our jackets, caps and gloves and opened the door. We stepped out into the bright but cold afternoon sunlight.

Santa was standing there, hands on his hips, with a broad smile. "Welcome to the North Pole!" he said in a booming voice.

He was just as I had envisioned he would be, only somehow bigger and more charismatic.

We loaded my bags into the sleigh. "How do you like my rig?" Santa asked, pointing to the large shiny red sleigh and the team of beautiful reindeer.

It was a fantastic rig in many respects. But the thing that really got my attention was that he had bumper stickers. Yes, bumper stickers! Like "Children are Little People" and "Hugs not drugs."

"Wow," I said. "It's really cool."

He slapped me playfully on the back, and said "Let's do it."

I got in on the passenger's side and fastened my seatbelt. Santa jerked the reins and commanded each reindeer individually. The sleigh glided forward slowly at first but steadily gained speed. Within a couple hundred yards, the reindeer rose upward and we were airborne!

Santa was very focused, working the reins as we headed due south, ascending to an altitude of about 300 feet. Santa began pulling on the left rein and we banked to the left, making a gradual 180 degree turn. As we made the turn, I saw the weather scientists below waving to us.

I waved a final goodbye as we began a steep climb, now heading due north. I knew I was in for quite a ride.

- 1 -

Letter Spurs Santa to Speak Out

Santa was pacing back and forth in his office, clutching a letter in his hand.

Every two or three rounds of pacing, he would pause by the window for a few seconds, staring out at the snowy winter landscape, and then start pacing back and forth again.

Mrs. Claus quietly snuck up the stairs. She had heard the creaking of his boots overhead from her rocking chair in the living room where she did her knitting.

She stood by the office door and watched him pacing. Finally, she said in a gentle voice (so as not to startle him), "What's wrong, Dear?" (She called him Dear.)

Santa turned and saw the concern in her face. He came over and took one of her hands, putting it between his. He gently patted her hand with his, and with a warm smile, said: "Oh, I guess I just worry too much."

"What is it?" she inquired. "You're not having supply problems at the factory again, are you?"

"No," Santa replied. "It's today's parents. I just don't know what they are thinking."

He paused for a moment, and then continued.

"I just got a letter from Caitlin, my 7 year old friend in Boston. You know, the one who got an A on her math test . . ."

Mrs. Claus nodded. Her eyes began to twinkle. "She's the one who asked you to bring an iPad for her mom."

"Well," continued Santa, "her mom has been making her stay in her room for 30 minutes at a time," and then shaking his head sadly, he said, "or even longer!"

"Oh, for heaven's sake, why?" asked Mrs. Claus.

"Because she didn't pay attention. Then because she spilled some milk on her dress." Santa waved the letter in the air and said, "Yesterday she got an hour for interrupting her dad. They told her to stay in her room and make a list of things she will do in the future instead of interrupting, but she was so upset all she could do was cry."

Then Santa fell silent.

"I'm sorry," said Mrs. Claus. "She's such a nice girl. What else did she say?"

Santa sunk in his leather chair. "She said she is angry at her parents, which makes her 'bad.' So since she is 'bad,' she told me not to bring her anything this year."

"Oh, no!" said Mrs. Claus.

Santa went to his desk and pulled at a big stack of letters.

"Every one of these letters mentions this new 'time out' thing. I'm making a little graph on the computer. I've been looking at emails and letters and keeping a careful record of what the children say about the length of the time outs. Over the past 12 months, the average length of a time out has increased by 6.5 minutes!"

He went back over to his chair and once again sat down in a slump.

Mrs. Claus quietly dusted some crumbs from the computer table. "I'll make some tea," she said.

"I wish I could get the word out to parents about how awful these time outs can be."

"I know," Mrs. Claus said sympathetically. "But we certainly don't want parents to go back to spanking."

"No, we don't want that," Santa muttered. "If only they knew that there are viable alternatives which are both effective and fun."

"You mean like your favorites-- huddling, high fives, and hugs?"

"Yes, yes! Precisely," Santa said forcefully. "But how can I get the word out?"

Mrs. Claus paused at the door.

"Why don't you contact that nice man Rupert who you talked to yesterday about coming up for an interview? Tell him to go ahead and start researching the time outs issue. It will help him get a head start. You guys can correspond by email and then talk about it more when he is here next month."

Santa was lost in thought. But after a few seconds, as if he had just heard what Mrs. Claus said, he stood up and announced:

"I'll do just that. It's not Rupert, it's. . . . . . Rudolph, no . . . . . Roland, that's it."

He went to the computer. "I've got him on my contacts list. I'll tell him to be sure to write a whole chapter about time outs."

Mrs. Claus was already on her way to make tea.

$$* \qquad * \qquad *$$

Roland was in his office sitting at the computer. His wife, Sophia, was in the living room.

"Sophia, I just got an email from Santa. He wants me to write a whole chapter on time outs."

"What did you say, Dear?" Sophia said loudly so her voice would carry down the hallway, around the corner, through the office door and past the earphones Roland had on seemingly all the time.

Roland cupped his hands and yelled: "I got an email from Santa!"

"How's he doing?" Sophia asked, putting down a book she was reading.

"He's okay," Roland said. "He wants me to write a whole chapter on time outs."

"For or against?" Sophia yelled back.

"Against," Roland mumbled as he double clicked on his book document.

"And that suits me just fine," he continued. "I'm not a big fan of time outs either."

"What did you say?" Sophia asked.

A Short and Informal History of Time Outs

When I was a kid (a long time ago), it was "Go to your room!" This was usually stated with the mandatory obligatory stern voice. Frequently, the parent chose to add an outstretched arm held rigid and horizontal with the index finger pointing toward the room.

There were occasionally additional instructions or warnings issued, and a parent would sometimes add in certain circumstances, "And don't come out until you are sorry."

Being banished to one's room usually ended when the next meal (often dinner, for some reason) was served. The whole family was seated and the guilty party arrived and sat in his or her chair with head down. Food was put on his plate and he was required to eat it. Often there was a conversation between the parents, with the other parent inquiring: "What did he/she do?" The other kids looked at each other and at the parents. They were required to look serious. They were not allowed to giggle.

If mom was the one who carried out the sentence of banishment, then dad, after being briefed on what the child had done, would have to add mandatory additional lecturing or warnings. It was usually something along these lines: "If I ever come home again and find out that you.........(fill in the blank), then I'll ....(fill in the blank with some punishment administered by him personally)."

There were many variations of the above scenario, some involving an argument flaring up between the parents. If the infraction occurred in the evening, then it was "brush your teeth and go to bed."

But there was always a happy ending. When the meal was over, it was usually back to business as usual. And don't forget--way back then in antiquity, most families had four, five, six, or more kids. So it wasn't long before another sibling did something wrong, and what the original guilty party did was quickly forgotten as attention was now focused on the new offender.

When the evening variation ("brush your teeth and go to bed") was implemented, it often ended with the door opening and a parent quietly coming to sit down on the edge of the bed. There was a gentle admonishment, followed up by being tucked in with perhaps a good night kiss.

Let me say a word about the daytime version of the banishment to one's room. As a kid, I considered it a punishment only if there was something good on the television that I would miss, or if the other kids got to go outside and play.

Otherwise, frankly, and especially for the only child, being sent to one's room was often a welcome relief. Since there was no assigned duty to perform, I looked at my baseball cards or listened to the radio. Plus my mom couldn't keep yelling at me when I was in the safe haven of my room.

The next evolution of "go to your room" was the addition of mandatory stern preconditions and warnings.

For example: "Don't come out until your homework is done. And don't let me catch you looking at your baseball cards or listening to the radio." Still, the punishment was manageable; although it did become dicier when "just wait till your dad gets home" was added.

Those were the good old days. Now things are different.

The go-to-your-room card parents used to play is apparently no more. Today it's "time outs."

The trouble is: there is no sense of humor in these new time outs. It's like zero tolerance. It's a power play, but one in which the parent admits inadequacy and compensates with a combination of avoidance and arbitrariness.

To be fair, it must be stated that there is one big thing that time outs have in their favor—they replace spanking. I will be the first to admit that I am glad to see the change in attitude toward spanking. Today spanking is generally frowned on.

I am opposed to spanking, and so I am glad that many, if not hopefully, most parents are not spanking their kids. I, for one, don't want to go back to the days of spanking anymore than I want a return to smoking in offices and restaurants.

I don't approve of spanking, period. I'm also not a fan of "go to your room." But as far as alternatives go, I just can't get comfortable with time outs.

"Okay, Roland," some of you are saying, "we get it. We understand that you are uncomfortable with time outs. Now please tell us why you don't like time outs."

First, let me say that I am on your side. I want you to succeed and I want to empower parents. That's one of the reasons why I've had to rethink time outs. I can see that time outs actually dis-empower parents. Here's why.

The most powerful force on earth for good is love. If you don't believe me then just ask Santa. Think back to when someone withdrew their love by shunning, rejecting, or growing cold toward you. It felt terrible, didn't it? What the parent has to remember is that being sent away to one's room to be alone and separated from the parent may feel like the parent is withdrawing love.

Chances are you may just be trying to de-escalate a situation by sending the child to their room. But to the child, it may be interpreted as "you don't love me." It may also be interpreted as "I am a bad person and made mommy so angry she can't deal with me anymore."

As a parent, you have a natural bond with your child. If love comes through this bond, then it is a powerful builder of self-esteem, security, confidence, hope, and self worth in the child. When it is absent, or *appears* to the child to be absent, it breeds fear, self-deprecation, insecurity, and low self-esteem.

To the child, being sent away at the drop of a hat feels like being shunned or even rejected. Some children will grow hard and inured to it. They will hate the parent and grow callous. The time out will mean nothing to them anymore, other than reaffirming a reason to hate the parent.

But before the child grows cold and indifferent, many children will experience big time separation anxiety. As previously stated, they may feel shunned and rejected.

Another problem is that the time out often includes instructions to the child to come up with some strategy or plan to better handle the situation in the future. Many kids, and especially little kids, just don't have the resources to do this by themselves. They need a parent to be there to help them with this task and guide them in the process. That's what a parent is for.

Without a parent's help in coming up with a plan, it only increases a child's anxiety. In fact, the whole time out thing can drive kids to one of two extremes: some become hardened; others become more timid, insecure, and fearful.

A final point--remember how I said that time outs dis-empower the parent? I showed how time outs disconnect parent and child, putting a physical and emotional distance between parent and child. In today's day and age, the *last* thing you want to do is put any impediment in the connectivity between you and your child.

The second reason why it is dis-empowering is this: children desperately and deeply need to see their parent as calm, as competent, and as able to handle things. A parent who sends the child off in time outs is literally saying: "I can't cope, I can't deal with you, and I can't help you. Go away and figure it out for yourself."

Could there be some other options—options that avoid the extremes of neglect, punishment, and permissiveness?

Could there be problem solving solutions that promote and foster connectivity and engagement, facilitate communication, and build, instead of threaten, bonds?

- 2 -

Santa's Take on Time Outs

"Helloooooooooo," the cheerful resonant voice boomed from the other end of the line.

"Hello, Santa, how are you?"

"Fine, fine."

I could picture Santa sitting in his leather chair, with his shoes off and his feet on the ottoman. He undoubtedly had on his red, green, and white striped socks which always appear to be about three sizes too big.

"Santa," I said, pausing to shuffle my notes, "we need to discuss the book."

"Go ahead," said Santa.

"I'm going to be honest with you. A lot of parents rely on time outs. And frankly, it is often recommended to them. Their thinking is that a time out is better than a spanking.

"I know you are not a fan of spanking," I continued. "I'm with you there. You and I are also on the same page about the potential drawbacks of time outs. I believe that time outs suggest that the parent can't cope, and this undermines a child's confidence in the parent.

Secondly, I think that time outs harden some kids while making others fearful and insecure. That's why I just don't think they are the answer."

"Yes, yes," Santa said.

"But," I said tentatively, "having said all that, I know that many parents rely on them. These parents are going to ask you, 'if we don't spank and we don't do time outs, then what should we do?'"

"Of course," said Santa. "That's why I called you to write the book. I'm going to tell you! Why, we haven't even scratched the surface yet."

I have to admit I gave a tremendous sigh of relief. Santa, as usual, was two steps ahead of me.

Santa laughed, and I know his eyes were twinkling.

"As soon as you arrive, I'll give you my take on time outs."

Time Outs Santa Style

Santa, Mrs. Claus, and I sat in silence for about three minutes. Then we all began to speak at the same time. It was really funny. We all laughed heartily. It was a great tension breaker.

Then another 30 seconds of silence followed by another round of laughter.

"Look at us! We're supposed to be these great communicators, and here we are sitting around like bumps on a log!" Mrs. Claus said jokingly.

"Dear," she said, "why don't you tell Roland about huddles, hugs, and high fives?"

"Yes, please, tell me more," I added.

"It's simple," said Santa. "Parents just need to tweak their time outs. You see,

I'm not really opposed to time outs, but mine are only 60 seconds or 2 minutes long at the most."

Santa sat back contentedly, as if he was waiting for me to be surprised and impressed by what he said.

But I just sat there with a puzzled expression on my face.

Santa took pity on me, laughed, and asked, "Do you watch basketball?"

"Yes," I said tentatively.

"Do you know what a time out is in basketball?"

"Yes," I said. Now the light was beginning to dawn. "You mean, when you have an issue with your kids, you call a time out like in a basketball game?"

"Now, you're cooking," Santa said.

"And your time outs last 60 seconds or 2 minutes?"

"You got it," Santa said.

"What do you do during the time out?"

Santa looked at me as if I were kind of dumb.

"You huddle," he said. "And you quickly make a plan, and the kids help you make the plan."

"Then you hug or high five?" I asked.

"Yes," said Santa. "You hug or high five and then spring into action."

"It's fun," Mrs. Claus added. "With little kids, you usually join in and do whatever the plan is for them to do. That way they can see how it's done."

"Let me make sure I understand where you're coming from," I said slowly. "So it's not a punishment--it's more like a sports huddle to come up with a play?"

"Right," said Santa.

"Sp it's short--like a minute or two--and the parent (as coach) is right there with the kids?" I asked with less hesitation, as I was beginning to get it.

"Yes," said Santa.

"You're all on the same team and if you come up with a cool play (plan), the whole team wins?"

"Bingo," said Santa.

"The opponent is not a person but the issue that coach and players are dealing with?" I was on a roll now.

"You got it."

"So it's not a parent vs. child thing. It's a team working on coming up with a plan

36

to deal with the issue? And it's fun because there is an element of play in it?"

"That's right," said Santa warmly.

I pondered what I had just learned for a moment, then said, "Okay, I get it. Can I ask just a couple more questions?"

"Of course!" Santa said cheerfully.

I continued, "Does it have to be exactly 60 seconds, two minutes or whatever?"

"No," Santa said warmly, "as long as it's like a sports huddle."

"Can only the coach call a time out or can the players . . . . I mean, kids . . . call time outs too?"

"Anyone can call a time out," Mrs. Claus joined in.

"I'll give you an example," she continued. "Santa taught his huddle, hug and high five system to a family where the mom had a little anxiety issue.

"When mom was a little girl, her mother would get angry and yell at her if she didn't make her bed, if she forgot to do a chore, or when she spilled something. So now when something happens that is like when mom was a child, she begins to feel anxious. If she starts raising her voice, the kids call a time out. And everyone gets together to support mom while she 'catches her breath.'"

"You mean like an injury time out in a game?" I inquired.

"Yes," said Mrs. Claus. "After mom is better, they then use the remaining time to deal with the issue (forgotten chore or whatever)."

"That's really cool," I said.

"I think so," Santa said proudly. "It gets the Santa Seal of Approval."

"Can you give me an example of how you guys have used a time out?" I inquired.

Mrs. Claus thought for a moment.

"Dear, why don't you tell Roland about how Kylie and Jonathan were leaving their rooms messy all the time."

"Sure," said Santa. "As you know, Kylie and Jonathan are great kids, but they had a habit of leaving their rooms messy. You know--bed not made, stuff lying on the floor, desk cluttered and so on. I kept reminding them. It got to the point that I was reminding them five or six times a day."

"And sometimes the bed still wasn't made all day," Mrs. Claus remarked.

Santa smiled and rolled his eyes. "So much for my authoritative manner," he laughed.

"But you didn't get angry," Mrs. Claus noted.

"No, but I was stern a couple of times," said Santa.

"Did they get upset or scared when you were stern?" I asked.

Mrs. Claus laughed. "When Santa is stern," she said, "his voice is stern but his eyes are still twinkling. So nobody gets scared. But they do know that he means business," she added. "If you don't believe me, just ask the two elves that got fired."

"Anyway," Santa said, "after several days of reminders, I called Kylie and Jonathan over. I clapped my hands and said, 'Coach Santa is calling time out to deal with this messy room situation.'

"The kids knew it was time to pretend they were on the basketball court, but also time to make some real plans. Kylie and Jonathan came up close and got down on one knee, leaning forward. I pulled the ottoman over and sat down on it.

"The three of us huddled together. 'What do we do about the messy rooms?' I asked.

'Start yelling at us?' Jonathan asked.

'I don't think so,' said Kylie.

'Punish us by making us shovel all the snow off the landing strip,' Jonathan said breathlessly.

'Get serious,' Kylie said authoritatively.

'I got it,' said Kylie, how about a fine for a messy room?'

'Might work. What do you think, guys?' I asked, just like a coach.

'Works for me, works for me,' they both said.

"I had to think fast (time was running out). 'I got it,' I said, snapping my fingers. 'Any one of us can call for an inspection at any time. When an inspection has been called, we all inspect my office and each of your bedrooms. The person with the messiest room has to pay everyone else a quarter.'

'Yaaah,' Jonathan said.

'Sure,' Kylie said.

"I clapped my hands and we all high fived."

"Tell them what happened the next day," Mrs. Claus said.

Santa continued: "The next afternoon, when Mrs. Claus and I were walking down the hallway I saw that their rooms were a mess. So I whispered to Mrs. Claus (using a loud stage whisper), 'in 10 minutes I'm calling for an inspection.'

"Of course they over-heard me. They both rushed to make their beds, get stuff off the floor and straighten their desks. I pretended not to notice.

"Meanwhile I quietly went to the kitchen and grabbed a banana. I peeled the banana and had a nice snack on the way to my office. I proceeded to spread a few papers on the floor and then dropped the banana peel right in the middle of my desk. Kerplunk.

"Ten minutes later I went to the living room and yelled 'room inspection.' The kids came running. I pretended to be very serious as we went up the stairs. First we examined Kylie's room. Result: neat and tidy. I acted surprised and puzzled.

"Then we looked at Jonathan's room. Perfectly neat. Again, I looked surprised.

"'Now, let's look at *your* office, Santa,' they said.

"'No problem,' I said, acting confident and poised--until we arrived at my office and they found papers on the floor and a banana peel on my desk! They both laughed with delight. They stuck their hands out.

"'Twenty five cents, Santa,' they said in unison. I acted as if I just couldn't believe what had happened as I dug two quarters out of my pocket."

- 3 -

Santa's Secret: The Power of Pretend

This is one of Santa's favorites. It's really popular with kids and with parents who give it a try. It may require a learning curve, since most parents are out of practice when it comes to pretending. But Santa believes that many, if not most, garden variety issues can easily be dealt with when mom or dad uses "the power of pretend." Kids love to play and pretend. It is so much fun for them when mom or dad joins right in. Not only is it fun, but it makes otherwise not fun issues become fun.

Let's begin with a situation that Mrs. Claus told me about. Her grandkids were visiting. Three in total. They played and had fun all day, but now it was 8:30 which was time for them to brush their teeth and start getting ready for bed.

Oh, incidentally, the Clauses do not think that little kids should be up late, and so at the Claus residence, all children are in bed between 8:00 and 9:00. "A good night's rest is always best," says Santa.

Anyway, the grandchildren were having such a good time, they did not want to stop playing and go brush their teeth. Mrs. Claus reminded them several times, but they kept stalling. Finally, Mrs. Claus said, "Oh dear!"

"What is it, Grandma?" they asked.

"I believe I have some of that taffy we ate earlier stuck between my teeth. Oh, what am I going to do?"

"Brush your teeth," they exclaimed.

"But I don't want to," Mrs. Claus replied, crossing her arms and pouting.

The children looked at each other, and then one said: "You have to."

"But it's dark in the bathroom," Mrs. Claus said.

"Don't worry, we'll take you," they exclaimed.

Mr. Claus was in his office reading. Suddenly he heard footsteps in the hallway, almost like marching. Then he looked through the open office door and saw a parade of four people marching by. One child was in the lead, another was holding Mrs. Claus's hand, and two were bringing up the rear.

Then everything became quiet. After a few minutes, Santa grew curious and tiptoed down the hallway to see what was going on.

Around the corner, he saw the light on in the bathroom. Four people were crowded around the sink—three children and Mrs. Claus—all brushing their teeth! He inched closer and heard one child say, "Grandma, it's a good thing we are here to show you how to brush your teeth properly. The way you were doing it was all wrong!"

Santa chuckled and tiptoed back to his office.

Email
From: Santa
To: Roland
Re: Chapters 1, 2, and 3

Thanks for sending me a draft of the first 3 chapters. I found the short description of the evolution of time outs fascinating.

I never interfere in a parent's choices. Like I've always said: "I don't raise the girls and boys, I just bring the toys!"

Nevertheless, your book gives me an opportunity to help parents out a little.

Since I get so many letters from children, I get to read what kids are experiencing and feeling. I see patterns developing I think I can help with. With a little bit of coaching from me, a little feedback, and some fresh approaches, I think most parents can make some little adjustments that will result in big improvements in how they get along with their kids.

I know it's tough being a parent nowadays, so I'm definitely pulling for the parents to succeed.

I'm not a writer. That's why I've asked for your help. You'll be able to put it all together in a little book, like a gift book, that parents can enjoy reading and give to each other.

My hope is that I can help parents and kids worldwide love each other, get along better, and be successful too.

Incidentally, Mrs. Claus was delighted that you included the story she told you.

Just a couple suggestions. Don't forget to mention that sometimes a hug is the "best medicine" for an unhappy child. A rebellious, angry child is an unhappy child. The child is trying to tell the parent something. I get many letters and emails from children who tell me that mommy or daddy is angry with them for being bad. I don't think that parents realize just how devastating it is for kids when mommy or daddy is angry at them (or acts disappointed in them).

I'm not trying to tell you how to write your book, but please tell parents not to get angry in the first place. It just breaks my heart to see children think they are no good because mommy is angry with them.

Oh, and one more thing. Don't forget to mention how awful it is to lock a child outside or make them stay outside and not let them in. I just don't know how this practice got started, but it is an insidious thing.

Several little children have told me that their parent got angry at them because they woke up and started singing or talking at night. So the parent put them outside in the dark to punish them and make them stop.

Please tell the parents not to put their child out in the night or lock them out. It is so terrible. Waking up and talking, laughing or singing is something that little kids sometimes do. It's a phase they go through. Perfectly normal. I did it too when I was a kid.

Anyway, keep up the good work.
Santa

From: Roland
To: Santa

Your feedback is much appreciated. I hope your comments remind parents of what it is like to be a child.

I would like to add that parents don't realize that they already have the authority. So threatening or getting angry is unnecessary. A child naturally looks up to his or her parent. All the parent has to do is use their natural authority with gentleness and kindness. Because anger lacks love, it actually diminishes a parent's authority.

Thanks,
Roland

- 4 -

Santa's Secret: Have a Light Touch

Kylie and Jonathan had only been visiting Santa and Mrs. Claus for three days when the incident happened. The following is pieced together from what Santa told me and from what Kylie and Jonathan had to say when I interviewed them.

Here's what happened. Kylie asked Jonathan if he had an eraser she could borrow. Jonathan, who was looking at some of the books on Santa's living room shelves, ran to his backpack to get one for her. He began to pull on the zipper, but it was stuck.

"Oh, no," he muttered to himself, "not again." He kept pulling on it, growing more and more frustrated. Kylie called from the other room, "What's taking so long?"

"The zipper's stuck," Jonathan said. She began to laugh at him.

Jonathan became very angry at the backpack. He picked it up with both hands and started banging it on the floor, over and over and over.

Santa passed by the hallway entrance to the living room as he was on his way to get the newspaper. He arrived just in time to see Jonathan banging the bag on the floor with tears in his eyes.

Santa stood by the door for a moment and let Jonathan bang the backpack three or four more times. Then he came over and gently but firmly took hold of the backpack. Jonathan struggled to wrestle it loose, as Santa quietly held it still. Jonathan let go of the backpack and reached out for a hug from Santa as he burst into tears. Santa put the backpack down and got down on one knee next to

Jonathan. "What's wrong, Jonathan?" he asked tenderly.

"I hate that bag. I hate it." Santa put his hand on Jonathan's shoulder. Still on one knee, he saw Kylie standing a few feet away with a grin on her face. Santa made a motion with his head, with an almost imperceptible furl of his brow that said "leave me alone with Jonathan, just now."

Kylie got the message and went back to her activities in the other room.

Jonathan was no longer sobbing, but was standing there very downcast.

Still on one knee, Santa looked Jonathan in the eyes (Jonathan later said it was a look of tenderness and "as if Santa were looking right through me").

Santa patted him on the shoulder. "Jonathan, can you help me out?"

Jonathan frowned as if to say, "What?"

"We just got a huge shipment and I need to verify the count of the number of pallets that just arrived. There are so many that I could use some help. If you could count the pallets of wrapping paper, then I can count the ones with boxes of ribbon. With your help the job will be done in half the time."

"Sure," Jonathan said.

Mrs. Claus was upstairs in her office when she heard the front door close. She looked out the window and saw Santa and Jonathan walking to the factory. Santa had his hand on Jonathan's shoulder and they were walking like a father and son. She watched them grow smaller in the distance as they made their way to the factory.

No one knows what was said, or if anything was said. Things don't always have to be said. Santa knew that Jonathan wasn't mad at the backpack. He was angry at his sister for laughing at him. Then he was angry at himself.

Jonathan later recounted that somehow the look Santa gave him made him aware that he shouldn't be angry at his sister. And somehow, and he can't say just how, he started to realize that with his dad gone, he was going to have to be the man of the family. Somehow, it just wasn't proper for the man of the family to act like he had been acting.

The next day, Santa took Kylie with him into town to get some items Mrs. Claus had ordered. They talked about many things--school, life, Mrs. Claus's birthday party, and even about the future.

To this day, Kylie does not remember their having talked about what happened the previous day, but somehow Kylie says that it wasn't long after that that she began to notice that she just didn't enjoy teasing Jonathan as much as before. In fact, a couple of years later they would become the best of friends.

- 5 -

Santa's Secret: The Power of Routine

I wish you could have been there. I was sitting at the Claus's kitchen table, with my yellow lined 8 1/2 by 14 notepad covered with cookie crumbs. Not to mention the crumbs on my lap. I was waving my hand back and forth saying, "No, please. I couldn't even dream of eating another."

And there was Mrs. Claus, laughing and placing another chocolate chip cookie on my plate.

But the best part was Santa. He was at the other end of the table, munching away, taking a sip of milk every other bite, and occasionally turning a page on his new e-book reader.

"One of the benefits of being Santa is that I get to try out some of the new merchandise." He was saying it absent-mindedly, totally oblivious to the fact that I had already eaten eight (yes, eight cookies), with more on the way.

Finally, Mrs. Claus had mercy on me, but muttering something about how I was "too skinny and not eating right," she brought a plate with six cookies on it, covered with clear plastic wrap.

"These are for when you get hungry later," she said matter-of-factly, while going to get a little brush and dustpan. She made me sit perfectly still and said, "Don't move," while she brushed me off.

Mrs. Claus sat down and began to check out Santa's e-book reader.

Santa brushed some crumbs off his vest, sat back contentedly in his chair, and said, "What would you like to interview me about now?"

Mrs. Claus laughed and said to me, "Ask him what his favorite type of cookie is."

Santa reached over and patted her hand tenderly. "Don't forget, Dear," he said, "we can't tell."

"Oh, I forgot," said Mrs. Claus.

"You see," said Santa, anticipating my question, "some parents don't allow their children to have cookies. Besides, if I mentioned my favorite type, then children everywhere would somehow find out and then ask their parents for that cookie. If the parents objected, the children would say 'Santa eats them, and if Santa eats them, they have to be good for you.' So you see--I have to be mum on the subject."

"I see," I said solemnly.

After a brief pause, I brought up something that had been on my mind for a long time. "As you know," I began, "lots of parents are experiencing hard times. Some are out of work or living in scary places. I'm sure the children mention it when they write you. What recommendations do you have for these parents?"

I expected Santa to stand up and pace back and forth, perhaps pausing to look wistfully out the window as he composed a philosophical answer to my question.

Instead his eyes twinkled, and he immediately leaned forward and announced, "I've got the title for a whole chapter in your book!"

Then he leaned back in his chair and sat smugly as if he had just accomplished an act of earth-shattering importance.

"Oh, don't be so dramatic," Mrs. Claus teased. "Tell the man the answer."

Santa put his hands on his tummy and laughed and laughed.

"The power of routine," he said.

"The power of routine?" I responded incredulously.

"Is there an echo in here?" Mrs. Claus said playfully.

"Totally," Santa said without a pause. "Listen, I tell you what, I've got to do my morning rounds—you know, say hi to everyone, answer any questions, inquire about work progress, and so on. Why don't you come with me? While we're walking I'll tell you what I have in mind."

Email
From: Roland
To: Santa
Re: Chapter 5, The Power of Routine

Please review at your earliest convenience. Remember when we went for your morning rounds, and you told me all about routine? Well, when I got back I found that my MP3 recorder battery had been low, so I didn't get any of the interview. I had to try to remember what you told me. Hope I got it right.

Here it is. Your comments will be greatly appreciated. I put it below in the body of the email. Roland

The Power of Routine

This principle is so simple that many parents miss it. It is so obvious that parents forget to remember it. And it is so mundane that, frankly, many parents forget to practice it.

But it can be a powerful helper for parents.

Routine has many subcategories, each of which is important in its own right. But I want to focus on the overarching principle, so that you see it clearly.

Kids like routine. They like to do the same thing every day, and at the same time and in the same way. They have their favorite spoon for eating cereal in the morning. They love to snack every afternoon at the same time. And they like to sit in the same chair after school, drink from the same cup and eat the same kind of cookie.

Most kids love to be read to at night before going to sleep. Many kids want to be read to from the same book, or even the same part of the book.

Or they want you to tell them the same story.

They have a favorite shirt or dress, a favorite doll or stuffed animal. They love for Daddy to say the same thing when he comes home, or Mommy to say the same thing when she arrives from work or running errands.

Since every child is unique and every family is special, you will have your very own list of things your child loves to do over and over.

Before I let you in on a very big secret to parenting success (I wish I thought of it, but Santa gave it to me), I want to spend a little more time emphasizing why routine is so important.

First, kids love it. Secondly, it gives them a sense of security. So if something brings them joy and gives them a sense of security, why not take advantage of it? Be grateful for it.

Routine is a gift to parents. I remember years ago when I was teaching business in college, my students talked about franchises--like McDonalds, Subway, or Starbucks. One of the reasons these franchises have been so successful is they develop a system that works and then they just do the same thing over and over again.

Customers get a consistent product with no surprises, employees can easily do the same thing over and over, and when crunch time comes (like a long line of customers), each employee knows exactly what to do.

So when your child goes to the same chair, gets the same toy, asks to be read to from the same book, etc., it makes it easy for you.

Here's where routine really becomes the parent's best friend—when it comes to daily tasks like making their bed, brushing their teeth, combing their hair, feeding the cat, putting out the garbage, and so on.

For example, a "getting up and getting ready" routine, a "setting the table" routine and a "clearing the table" routine, a "getting ready for bed" and a "goodnight" routine make the day fun and easy.

Now Santa wanted me to mention that he has been around for a long time (he wouldn't tell me how long). He's seen many bad situations around the world and he's seen hard times. He tells me that even when things are chaotic out in the world, if the parents are calm at home and maintain the daily routines, kids seem to come through just fine.

He also wanted me to mention that routine becomes really important when something big or different is happening to the family, like when someone goes into the hospital or a parent changes (or loses) a job. It could also be like when a distant relative comes to visit or the family goes on a big vacation trip. Santa says that maintaining routine is very important in any of these situations.

Change (even when it is fun) is stressful, so you always want to have plenty of routine to make any changes manageable.

Now, here's the special secret that Santa has permitted me to share. *A parent's reaction is also a part of the routine.* And kids will look forward to the parent's reaction and take delight in it.

For instance, getting kids to go to bed may require mom to say, "Okay, it's time to go to bed!" several times. Here's an example. Mom says it once. Five minutes go by. She says it again. Another five minutes elapse and she repeats it again.

Another five minutes pass and she says it yet again.

Now she yells from the living room up the stairs "Okay, go brush your teeth *right now!*" (Emphasis on the *right now.*) Nevertheless, five minutes later, she is bounding up the stairs, clapping her hands, and saying in a loud voice, "March!"

After this happens two or three evenings, it becomes a routine. The kids take great delight in knowing what is going to happen. They can predict each step of the process and they know that eventually mom will come up the stairs and say, "March!"

Now you know why they squeal with delight (with a pinch of mock fright) when they hear her coming up the stairs. They know she is going to say "March!" And they know that this time she means business.

Santa says that when mom says "march," 99% of the time the kids will now scramble to get ready for bed. Why? Because scrambling to get ready for bed when mom says "march" becomes part of the routine!

Here's another example. It could be that whenever the child asks for another cookie, Dad always rolls his eyes, and says, "No way."

Then three minutes later he always relents and says, "Well, okay, just one more. But this is the last one."

Do you see the fun for the kids? If the parent does not get angry or resentful, but just goes along good naturedly, playing his or her role in the routine, it's all good fun, like a comedy show.

Santa says that sometimes parents just have to pretend they are at the end of their rope. Kids are pretty smart. They know it's pretend, but they know it's also sort of real, so now they get the opportunity to be good sports and do what the parent wants. It's like a fun skit.

Some parents will object. They feel they have to be very serious and authoritarian, so as not to appear weak.

Santa says parents already have the authority. "Kids know who the parent is.

When you are kind instead of mean, they just love it."

I once had a very good boss who taught me a lot. I remember that whenever he gave me a tough assignment (or one I thought was tough), he always said "I'll never ask you to do something that I wouldn't do myself." I know he meant it because I saw him tackle tasks (when he was in his 50's) that would tax a man half his age. I respected him for that.

When you, as parent, brush your teeth, do your homework, make your bed, and so on—kids see it and they respect you for it.

If it's time for the little kids to brush their teeth, then brush yours at the same time. If you are asking them to do some homework, then pay some of your bills at the same time. Santa says you can even complain (or pretend to complain) about having to pay them. Then you can start to read a fun magazine, and when the kids notice that you are reading instead of working, they will remind you to finish your work first!

When you play along with your kids because you know it brings them joy, it makes you stand tall in their eyes.

In the study of business management, it is well known that some of the best and most respected bosses are the ones who take off their suit coat, roll up their sleeves, and go right down to the shop floor to work side by side with their employees.

Little kids love to play. "Playing is learning," Santa says, so you can be a great parent by just playing with them.

Santa says that parents already have the authority. Having fun does not diminish it.

I remember the movie *The Sound of Music* with Julie Andrews. When it came out I was a young teenager. I went to see it three times. I remember that when the nanny (played by Julie Andrews) arrived, the kids' dad was very rigid and serious; and no one was having any fun. Remember the joy she brought? Was she permissive? No way. But did she have a light touch and playful attitude? Yes.

Flash forward for just a moment to the day when the last child in your home will get married or go away to work in another town. See yourself sitting on the floor in their empty bedroom. No furniture, no posters on the wall. The closet is empty with no toys or clothes in it. Everything is gone, and now the laughter and the fun that you once knew there will be no more.

Now return to the present and see your child as the gift that he or she is. Cherish the golden moments in life. Kids grow up very quickly. Trust me.

A final note: Santa says, "Not to worry" that the routine will go on forever. Kids may want to be read the same thing or do the same thing over and over for days, weeks, or months. They want you to read a certain story to them every night for awhile. If so, just good naturedly read it to them. Then, mysteriously and without warning, one night they will just want to do something else.

A final note. If you are like many parents today, you may only have one child. If so, everything Santa and I have said applies even more so to you and your child. Since there are no other siblings at home (yet!), your child will need you to spend a little extra time playing with her.

You'll have plenty of chances to practice your pretending skills as you blend some good old fashioned fun into chores and work.

Other parents will marvel at how good your relationship is with your child and why you don't have the problems that they have. Santa knows.

Email
From: Santa
To: Roland
Re: Chapter 5

Looks good. Thanks!

I just have one concern. When the parents read about routine and how important it is to a child, they may think that there is no place for a surprise. But of course, children love surprises. No one knows that more than I. So you better put in a chapter about surprises.

Remember? We talked about "surprises that are not surprises but are still surprises?"

Santa

Email
From: Roland
To: Santa
Re: Surprises that are not surprises but are still surprises

Yes, I remember. I'll be sure to include this topic.

- 6 -

Santa's Secret: Surprises that are not Surprises but are still Surprises

This chapter is about the phenomenon known as "the story book paradox." Every parent knows that every kid has something that he or she wants you to do over and over again. For example, many kids like to be read to every night. Of course, this is part of the routine that kids like.

But some kids want to be read the same story over and over. And they still take delight in hearing it. Most kids' stories contain fun surprises. But after you've heard it more than once, it becomes a surprise that is not a surprise but is still a surprise.

How can this be? You just have to remember what it is like to be a child to understand.

Parents tend to forget what it is like to be a kid. However, if you remember what it is like to be a kid, then you will begin to develop understanding. Your heart will soften, and you will relate to your child so much better.

Maybe this will help. How many of you have told your favorite joke over and over? The punch line is not really a surprise because you've told it so many times, yet it still makes you laugh.

How many of you know someone who tells the same funny joke over and over? You've heard it before, and they are telling someone who hasn't heard it but you are there listening. Yet, it's still fun. You can't help but smile. You know what is coming. You know everyone is going to laugh. You know that you are going to laugh. As you listen, you anticipate the punch line and begin to smile. There it is, and the laugh you've been holding in breaks forth.

It's the anticipation, you say. Okay, you're right. But there's more to it. How can you be surprised by something you know is coming? Here's the answer: the surprise has an element of pretend in it. You pretend you don't know what is coming (even though you do).

But because you know what is coming, you can feel secure. That is the second important aspect: the security of knowing what is coming.

For example, you don't mind going on an amusement park ride and being "scared," because you know you are going to be okay. You don't mind watching a bad guy do something wrong on an old Lone Ranger Show because you know good will triumph in the end.

Many people enjoyed watching Johnny Carson tell jokes or Ed McMahon making remarks on the old Tonight Show because they knew it would be good clean fun. The jokes were good natured and clean; they poked fun at themselves more than anything. You didn't have to worry that there would be bad language or something in poor taste. Therefore, you could relax and enjoy the show.

One more example. Remember going on a fun family vacation? The sights were surprises but the trip was safe. Dad was driving. Mom was there. You felt secure sitting in the back seat, looking out the window and seeing all the fun things going by.

Combine anticipation, security, and safety, and you have a winning combination.

Therefore, dear parents, have some fun. Pretend a little. Kids take great delight when mom always misplaces her pen (but it's behind her ear). The kids know it's behind her ear (but mom pretends that she doesn't know). Then she is surprised when she finds it behind her ear. It's great fun.

Kids love it when dad starts telling what a great free throw shooter he used to be, and then takes careful aim with a rolled up piece of paper at the waste basket. He then misses by a mile. The kids know he is going to miss but he doesn't know (he pretends he doesn't know). When he misses, he acts like it's a big surprise.

One dad I know always brought something for the kids. Every time he went to work, went to the store, or ran some errand, he always brought something home for the kids.

If there had been free samples of pastry at Starbucks, he brought one home, wrapped in a napkin. If he drove by the thrift store, he bought an old *Highlights for Children* magazine or a small toy. If he went to the office, he brought home a cookie or the newspaper sports section (when the boys got older).

Nobody knew just what he would bring home, but they knew he would bring s*omething.* He made it into a double surprise by coming through the door empty handed. Then he suddenly said, "Oh, I almost forgot," and he reached into his pocket, and there was something there.

Parents, here's your homework assignment: have fun. One thing Santa emphasized is that the parenting should be fun. Don't rely on the television, the video game, the toy, the pizza parlor, or the food to provide the fun. Let your loving, light hearted cheerful presence be the fun. The thoughtful little things you do and being easy to be with will bring joy to your kids.

Email
From: Santa
To: Roland

Good chapter. I think maybe I'm becoming a kid again. I like to do the same things over and over. Mrs. Claus likes change more than I do. In fact, she wants to go on a cruise. Maybe I'll surprise her!

- 7 -

Santa's Secret: The Power of Love

One late afternoon, I accompanied Santa as he made his rounds to different work stations in the factory. As we walked he talked and began to tell me about Jonathan and Kylie.

Jonathan and Kylie came to stay with Santa and Mrs. Claus four years ago. Altogether, they stayed for eight months. Santa never did tell me just how it all came to happen, but he did relate the following to me, as I was sitting beside Santa in the sleigh as we were rushing back home to avoid an approaching storm. It was noisy and I missed some of the details. But I will recount it as best I can.

Jonathan and Kylie were brother and sister. Jonathan was 5 and Kylie was 6.

Jonathan basically would run from one end of the room to the other. He would play with one toy for five minutes and then abandon it for another. He would suddenly get up and look through all the drawers or pull books off the shelf. He liked to throw things—his shoes, his socks, books, just about anything.

Kylie would not play with her brother. She sat by herself and talked to an imaginary friend. If Jonathan seemed angry about something, Kylie seemed sad about something. Though they were both smart, neither was doing well in school.

There were some issues between their parents—their mom and dad were recently separated.

Santa happened to be very busy at the time they arrived, and so was Mrs. Claus. Preparations for the forthcoming Christmas season were in full swing and this was a particularly intense year. Santa informed me that Mrs. Claus is generally just as busy as he is, since she supervises most of the administrative functions.

The bottom line, according to Santa, is they just didn't have a lot of time to spend on the two kids.

Santa explained to the kids that both he and Mrs. Claus were very busy and said that he would not have much time to devote to them. But he took Jonathan with him all day, and Mrs. Claus had Kylie with her while she worked.

Santa put in long days on the phone, going to the factory, holding meetings with the supervisory elves, going to town, and working on the computer. Every day he devoted himself to work, and Jonathan tagged along. In fact, some of the elves joked that Jonathan must be Santa's shadow because wherever Santa was, there was Jonathan.

Sometimes Jonathan would watch what Santa was doing. Sometimes Jonathan just played by himself while Santa was busy. Sometimes they did the same thing, like counting toys or looking up addresses.

Sometimes Jonathan pretended to do what Santa did. Jonathan even began to carry his own clipboard, just like Santa did. Other times Jonathan was in the room where Santa was—but while Santa worked, Jonathan read or did school lessons from his workbook.

Mrs. Claus reports much the same thing. She had so much to do that she hardly had time to pay attention to Kylie. Mrs. Claus put in long days both at home and helping supervise in the factory. Nevertheless, everywhere she went, Kylie was with her: sometimes helping, sometimes playing, sometimes reading.

When we arrived back at Santa's home, I took off my gloves, boots, cap, and heavy coat. I put on a sweater, washed my hands, and then sat down by the fireplace in the living room.

I never knew what to expect for dinner. I discovered that the Clauses love food from all over the world. One night they would have spaghetti, the next burritos, then maybe some kind of rice dish, or shish kebab. I smelled something good, and couldn't wait to find out what it was.

"Dinner's ready," Mrs. Claus called out cheerfully. Santa and I sat down at the kitchen table. Mrs. Claus always insisted that Santa first have a salad and then some homemade soup before the main course. I had some too. My eyes grew wide as Mrs. Claus brought in tonight's dishes: broiled chicken, baked potato, Brussels sprouts, hot baked bread, butter and honey. It was pure heaven.

As we sat eating, Santa noted, "Chicken is Jonathan's favorite food."

"Kylie loves bread with just a little butter and lots of honey," said Mrs. Claus.

"Roland, I began telling you about Kylie and Jonathan," Santa said after finishing a slice of bread. "I have a favor to ask of you. When you talk to Kylie and Jonathan, would you please ask them to accept our apologies for having been so busy when they were here that we pretty much ignored them."

"We still email each other often," added Mrs. Claus. "Jonathan is doing well in school. Kylie is playing volley ball and taking piano lessons. Their parents are considering getting back together again. Jonathan and Kylie's mom says the two kids have overcome or outgrown some behavior issues they had and are both happy."

Santa continued: "Like I told you, when I mentioned to them in an email that you were here to interview me about parenting, Jonathan and Kylie insisted that I give you their phone number so that you could talk to them."

"So please tell them that we wish we could have devoted more time to them, but we were just so busy," Mrs. Claus repeated.

After finishing my first four day stay with the Clauses, I made my way home and began to organize my materials to begin the book. I was hesitant to call Jonathan and Kylie. Frankly, I was somewhat afraid that they would say that Santa and Mrs. Claus had been too busy working and not been attentive (which is what the Clauses had insisted).

But an email from Jonathan and Kylie's mom arrived, requesting that I call *that* evening for a 4 party conversation: myself, Kylie, Jonathan and their mom.

I must say I had qualms, because if they had something negative to say about the Clauses, well, it would be unfortunate.

Thankfully, my fears were quickly dispelled. I wish I had a transcript of the phone call. All I can do is report the gist of what was said.

I was about to begin by apologizing on behalf of the Clauses, as they had instructed me to, but before I could say a word both kids began talking at the same time, "We love Santa and Mrs. Claus," they said.

"I'm happy to hear that!" I said. But since I'm writing a book, I wonder if you could tell me why?

"Because they love us," they said.

"How do you know?" I asked.

"Because they spent all their time with us."

"Santa took me everywhere," Jonathan said. "He showed me stuff. He asked me questions and told me all about making toys. He showed me how to do things and he was like my grandpa. I helped him look up addresses, and every day I helped him push the sleigh when the reindeer were unhitched.

"Sometimes when he was doing something, he would move aside and let me try. He explained why he did certain things a certain way instead of another. He talked to me like I already knew and he was just reminding me. He showed me how to use Word and Excel, and he let me type on Word when he was doing something else."

"Mrs. Claus let me help her on the computer too," said Kylie. "She put me in charge of managing and updating her contacts list. She also put me in charge of collating letters. It made me feel needed because collating, reading, and storing the letters Santa gets is very important.

"I learned all about office technology just by watching her. I was also there when one of her assistants brought an issue for her to solve.

"She told me all about what she was thinking when she was preparing dinner. I felt like I was her friend."

Soon their mom joined the conversation. She said that the Claus's "intervention" had given her her kids back and resolved many of their issues.

Then the kids began to tell me all the things they were doing now. At the end of the phone call, all agreed that every kid who has any issues should be able to spend time with the Clauses!

I have to tell you, despite all the years of counseling and all the books I had read on child rearing, I was temporarily at a loss to understand the meaning of what I had just heard.

Jonathan, Kylie and mom were insistent that the kids' visit with the Clauses was a very positive experience.

I was getting diametrically different takes on the visit. On the one hand, the Clauses insisted that they had been too busy to devote any attention to the kids, whereas on the other hand, the kids insisted that the Clauses had done just the opposite!

I processed the information for a couple days and I soon began to see that Santa and Mrs. Claus's success with the kids was a function of love. Just how this love works is a mystery, but *that* it works is certain.

The amazing thing is that, apparently, the person who has this love does not even sense that he or she has it! This is because this love is not a *feeling,* It is more like a quality that emanates from who one is deep down. It is like a sincere concern that is patient with others. It is a power to do good without even trying.

To the Clauses, their having the kids with them all day did not feel like love. But it felt like love to Jonathan and Kylie. Paying attention to important work and showing the kids duty and devotion in action didn't feel like love to the Clauses, but it felt like love to the kids.

Just having someone with you all the time while you go about your duties does not feel like love to you, but it often feels like love to the other person.

Taking someone with you and never acting like they are a bother does not feel like much to you. But it can feel like love to a child. Working, fishing or walking side by side are powerful because they are not confrontative, condescending, or contrived. Nor are they emotional. But they are very real.

Such is the power of love.

Another thing I began to see was that we are all capable of expressing this love that is deep within and which should naturally flow into everything we do. But where we fall short is when we let something interfere with the outflow of love. From what I have observed, anger and resentment appear to block the flow. It also seems to me that impatience blocks it. So does making our ego more important than what is right.

What Santa and Mrs. Claus did was a natural outflow of the good within them. They just basically never let selfishness, impatience, or anger get in the way. Everything they did had love in it.

For example, I saw that Santa and Mrs. Claus's love was expressed in watchfulness, attention to detail, caring for others, vigilance, doing their duty, and setting a good example.

This is part of the paradox of love. It is emotionless and it does not play favorites. The recipient of this emotionless love flourishes because he or she is not catered to or singled out for special praise or condemnation. Instead, the individual is given freedom within the context of good example and patience.

I began to understand it better when I related what Kylie and Jonathan had told me about the Clauses to some experiences I had had as a child.

If you are like me, you may have encountered this emotionless love, for example, if you had a rigorous teacher who was tough on everyone. You probably liked her fairness and learned a lot even though she didn't give you any special privileges.

Similarly, you may have had a coach or boss whom you liked even though he paid attention to the task and not to personality. He wanted to get the job done and demanded good performance and results. You liked honest assessment, constructive feedback, and attention to improving skill, rather than fussing over your feelings.

When I was a kid, I had some issues (as most kids do). I really disliked it when everyone was all concerned about my issues—worrying, fretting, analyzing, and talking to each other about me and my problems. The worst was when they felt sorry for me. What I liked was my friends, or certain coaches and teachers, who didn't feel sorry for me, but just let me be part of what was going on.

I liked it when people didn't know or care about my issues.

Here's a true story. At home I was criticized for being clumsy and unfriendly. I always felt like I was in the way.

But when I went to summer camp, no one knew I was clumsy or unfriendly. The bus driver who took all us kids to the camp was an expert at pitching horseshoes. He showed me how to throw them, and I soon found out I was good at horseshoes. A week later when he came back to get us, he watched me play horseshoes. I could see how proud he was of how well I was doing with his help. We chose up teams and my team beat his team!

For the first time in my life I felt like a real person who could excel at something. I felt like a person who had value and wasn't just getting in the way.

I have to admit there is a mysterious quality about love. It has an effect like the way sunlight makes plants grow or the way sunlight makes an old towel smell sweet. It's sheer magic.

Santa obviously has this quality. But you can too, and maybe already do.

We parents often feel like we have to find some technique or intervention to apply to our kids. Your kids don't want you to do anything to them (plenty of others are trying to do something to them). They just want you to be with them and be patient with them.

Email
From: Mrs. Claus
To: Roland

Mr. Claus is over at the factory (one of the conveyor belts broke and he and the foreman are working on it).

Santa and I were touched and a bit embarrassed to read all the nice things Kylie, Jonathan, and you said about us. I don't think we did anything special, but one thing I know for sure: Kylie and Jonathan are great kids.

I would like to make a suggestion. When it comes to parents' building relationships, setting a good example, and so on--tell them to start early.

It seems to me that this is important. Some parents are always gone or turning their kids over to daycare, preschool, and other activities to the point where they hardly spend any time with their kids. Parents and even the kids are so busy or distracted that family members are each living in their own world.

Maybe when the kids are older, like 17 or 18, I can see everyone being busy with work, school, sports and so on.

But I think parents should spend as much time as possible with their kids when they are little. I guess I'm old fashioned but for me, "little" means less than 12 years old!

From: Roland
To: Mrs. Claus

Thank you for your input. I will include your email in my book. Thanks

- 8 -

Santa's List

Santa sighed as he put down another letter. He stared out the window with a far away look and a touch of sadness. Then he stirred in his seat, sat up straight, and looked me in the eye. "You've got to get the message out," he said. "I'm counting on you."

Sensing the seriousness in his tone, I sat up straight too.

"Yes, Sir," I said.

"What do you want to cover next?" he asked in a matter-of-fact way.

I pondered a moment and then said, "The parents who read my book will fall into two categories. First are those parents (or parents to be) who want some proactive, preventative advice, so they can avoid some of the issues they see other parents dealing with.

"The second category of parents is those who are *already* dealing with parenting issues. Maybe, for example, their child is not listening to them, communication with their kids is poor, the kids are acting out, not doing well in school, or getting in trouble.

"I want to keep it all simple for them, and I don't want to take too much of your time. But I also want to make the advice yours, not mine."

"Yes, yes. Go on," Santa said enthusiastically.

"So," I continued, "I'm thinking maybe you could make two lists of Santa's suggestions for parents. Maybe a proactive (preventative) list. And another list for damage control."

I said the word "control" with a higher questioning tone. I certainly did not want to tell Santa what to do or impose on him by making him write lists.

I sat back in my chair, waiting for his response.

There were a few moments of silence, as he looked out the window.

I was about to say, ". . . . . but you are busy. You've given me plenty of your time already. I don't want to impose."

Just as I was about to speak, he clapped his hands together, and exclaimed:

"Great idea, Roland. I'll get started on the lists right now!" He bounded from his chair and went over to the computer. "I'll make a Word document. What do you like—single space or double space?"

"Single is fine," I said. Even as I spoke, he pushed his glasses up on his nose, wrinkled his forehead and began poking at the keys.

Mrs. Claus was passing by in the hallway. She came back to the doorway and peeked in. Observing Santa at the computer, she said, "What are you doing, Dear?"

"I'm making a list and checking it twice," Santa said. He leaned back in his chair, put his hands on his tummy and began to laugh. Mrs. Claus smiled and continued down the hallway.

Email
From: Santa
To: Roland

I completed the two lists: one list of things parents can do to help prevent issues from starting, and another list of things to do to help recover a good relationship with their child.

I need you to make what I wrote sound more scholarly or something. I always say things in simple terms like: play, having fun, being together, hugging, high fives, and such.

Yesterday when I finished the lists, I was about to save them when a pop up appeared and it was Word Readability Statistics. Word said I'm writing at grade level 5.6!

I was embarrassed. I know that the kids don't mind, but parents are used to bigger words and longer sentences. Would you please edit my lists and add some bigger words, so that adults will find my writing more acceptable?
Santa

Email
From: Roland
To: Santa

Santa, loving parents everywhere will find your writing perfectly acceptable. They care about the content not the grade level. But I'll do as you say. I'll expand some of your key concepts a little (but I'll keep it simple so kids can read it too!). Roland

- 9 -

Santa's Suggestions

Santa's proactive list

1. Start early to build a life-long relationship with your child. Spend as much time with your children as possible when they are small. Do things together. Have fun together.

2. Don't try to force your child to be nice or good. Just set a good example. He or she will see your example and it will make an impression. All kids will do naughty things. Don't expect them to be angels. Neither condone nor condemn. Patiently

correct error. Don't overly praise good behavior nor overly condemn mistakes.

3. Kids mimic. So be their number one model of behavior. Santa says:
"When your kids are little, be with them all the day, Always near as they eat, sleep, learn and play."

Note: Santa feels strongly about this one. Your kids are quick to mimic and fit in. If your kids spend time with you, they will conform to you. If they spend most of their time with others, they will conform to them.

Remember that kids will imitate what they see in daycare, on the street, in the video games, or on television. You should be the number 1 role model in your child's life. Not just qualitatively but also *quantitatively*. Put simply, your small child should see more of you and be more with you than with friends, sitters, teachers, television and video games *combined*.

4. Santa likes chores, reading, caring for a pet (even if it's just a goldfish), singing in choir, arts and crafts, playing a musical instrument, and working with mom or dad.

5. Have a home full of books. Santa says: "Mrs. Claus and I sit by the fire and read something from our living room library every evening. Sometimes we read out loud to each other."

6. Kids need quiet time. Kids need some time to play by themselves. Santa says he fully understands that kids need to be with others. But he says that today many kids spend the whole day in group settings. He says kids need a little creative time to play by themselves too.

By this Santa does not mean playing video games. He means playing with toys, drawing, coloring, making things, and enjoying hobbies like stamping, coin collecting, building models, and making scrapbooks.

7. Don't be too quick to fill their boredom. A child sitting on the floor in his bedroom with nothing to do (and no cell phone, video game, television, or personal music player handy) will reach for a book, grab some crayons, or dig the Legos out of the closet.

8. Careful of who you leave your kids with. Most people pretend to be nice, but not everyone is nice. Baby sitters, nephews, nieces, friends and even older siblings have been known to do something inappropriate, wrong or even dangerous when the parent is not present.

9. Listen to your kids. When Santa gets a letter from a child who says she is uncomfortable with someone who her parents insist on leaving her with, Santa tends to believe the child. (Santa is aware of the fact that kids have active imaginations. But when a child sounds the alarm bell, it is a parent's duty to pay attention and not just brush it off). Monitor your child's mood when he or she comes home from school or has been

with others. When in doubt, just do the simple and effective thing: remove your child from that environment. Don't leave your child alone with someone the child is uncomfortable with. Better safe than sorry.

Santa's Damage Control List

1. Start spending more time with your child. Many parents who are having issues with a teen, for example, discover that they and their teen live in different worlds. From morning to night, both are involved in so many activities with others that parent and child are never together.
If they are together, each is still in her own world: on the cell phone, on the computer, listening to music, or watching television. They are what Mrs. Claus describes as "side by side but worlds apart."

Santa doesn't know your particular circumstances, so Santa says you will have to figure out which activities keep the two of you apart and need to be cut back on or eliminated. Then you will have to come up with new activities you two can do together. Santa says to start with activities you will both enjoy.

2. Sometimes a big bold positive action is needed. Like changing jobs, working nights (so you can be with your child all day), or cutting back on your busy schedule to have more time to be with your child.

Sometimes you might need to be ready to get yourselves to a safe place. Santa received a letter from a nice 12-year-old girl who was anxious about going back to school because another girl was "mean" (in other words a vicious, cruel bully). Her mom considered all the options and decided to change schools. The new school environment was friendly and safe. Problem solved.

Another mom, facing similar issues, began home schooling. Her daughter quickly became happy again.

In another family, the kids were feeling pressure from nearby cousins who were gang members and taking drugs. Mom and dad decided to move the family far away. Dad found a job there, and the kids soon made new friends. "I don't want my kids being pressured," Dad said.

3. Just remember: you can't *build* a relationship apart. Later you can *maintain* one apart (more on this later), but you can't *build* one apart. First it has to be built together. Start to build a relationship that will last a lifetime by doing fun things together.

4. Find opportunities to just be together. Don't have an agenda (like "we're going to work on your behavior" or "I want to monitor you and your friends" or "I'm taking time out of my busy schedule to spend quality time with you"). Any such agenda will ruin it. Just be together. Don't

try to work on anything. Don't try to make something happen. Just be.

5. Make sure your kids are getting plenty of sleep. Mrs. Claus asked me to include this one. She has been on a campaign to get more sleep for kids. Mrs. Claus says that in her opinion, a large percentage of kids are just not getting enough sleep. They stay up late and then get up early. She says this is particularly the case with teens.

Santa says, "I think she is right. I can personally say that today many kids are just too busy. They need time to quietly play, to sit around relaxing (reading, for example). And they need plenty of sleep."

I was going to put this in the proactive list. Actually, it belongs in both lists. But I put it here in the damage control list because Mrs. Claus says, "I think that poor grades, listlessness, grouchiness, having trouble paying attention, and so on can sometimes be made worse by just being tired all the time. So if your kid is having some issues, start by making sure that he or she is getting ample rest."

6. Cut back on the junk food and the processed food. Santa admits, "I enjoy my snacks, but Mrs. Claus makes me eat fruit and vegetables too. She knows that when I'm working late in the workshop, I'll raid the cookie jar. So she makes sure I have good food at mealtimes."

7. Sometimes a pet can help. Especially if it is their pet. Santa has seen that many children have experienced betrayal, cruelty, and deceit at the hands of humans. But a pet is innocent and will not betray them, so the child can trust it.

8. A change of scenery can be good. Especially, for example, if you all go together to the country to visit your aunt who has a farm. If the new environment is wholesome and safe, then an extended stay is even better. And if there are things to do there—like chores or caring for animals--so much the better.

9. Any kind of helping others is good. Many times the focus of everyone is on

one child and *her* problem and *her* behavior. Such kids will often become self conscious and all concerned about themselves. An opportunity to help others gives them a chance to forget about themselves and render service to another.

10. Focus on what they *can* do, not on what they can't do. If a teen loves to skate, play the piano, or take photos, let her spend extra time on these. Don't always force the child to do what they can't do very well. Expect mistakes. Expect them to have their interests change.

Santa says that when he was a kid, he wanted to be a cowboy. When he was a tween, he wanted to be a baseball player. When he was a teen, he had no idea what he wanted to be.

11. Be available and be there, but don't TRY to help too much. I know this sounds like the opposite of what you would think I would say. I'm a big fan of families being together and having fun

together. I like to see parents busy and their child right beside them working, playing, watching, and learning.

But when something goes wrong, there is a tendency to try to force everything to be alright immediately. If this impulse is overdone, it leads to kids never learning to pick themselves up and dust themselves off. And it can lead to kids not having a chance to work through issues.

Since growing up and working through issues can take time--lots of time--trying to make everything better right away can lead to pressure on the kid and frustration for you. Frustration can then lead to basically quitting on your kids or turning them over to strangers for heavy handed or clumsy interventions.

Don't get me wrong. Be there. Be involved. Be connected. Be vigilant. Be ready to help. Be ready to get involved if they get in over their head. Be strong. Be ready to advocate for your child.

But don't forget that too much "help" can also lead to rebellion, where kids will go out into the streets just to be able to find something they can do themselves.

Look into your heart to find the right measure of helping and letting go. Also be aware that distrustful snooping around and false accusations will drive some kids to do the very thing you fear (the psychology is this: "since I've already been accused of it, I might as well do it.")

That's why kids seem to thrive in an atmosphere where there is a lot of work that has to be done. Everyone pitches in. No one is singled out or felt sorry for. Everyone just works. Kids like being useful and helpful, and not always being the focus of everyone's attention.

Email
From: Roland
To: Santa

I've attached the proactive list and the damage control list as a Word document so that you can edit it and make changes.

From: Santa
To: Roland

   Looks good. Mrs. Claus made a couple of small changes. Thanks.
Santa

- 10 -

Santa's Secret: Stay Close with Technology

Mrs. Claus awoke in the middle of the night. Santa was nowhere to be seen. She knew that he would sometimes go down to the kitchen to get a snack. She put her ear to the pillow and listened for the sound of the refrigerator door closing or the kitchen table chair scraping on the floor downstairs. But after a couple of minutes lying there and hearing nothing, she decided to get up and investigate.

She put on her cozy red robe and silver slippers and stepped out into the hallway. She saw a light coming through the crack from where the door was ajar to Santa's office. Quietly she stole down the hallway and peeked through the crack. Santa was at the computer, sitting behind the monitor, and she could see the light from the computer screen reflecting on his face.

He must have heard the floor creak because he looked up and peeked around the monitor. "What are you doing up?" he said.

"I came to see where you were," she said.

"Well, since you are up, come take a look," he said.

She walked around behind his desk and peered over his shoulder at the screen.

"This is Lincoln Jones's blog," he said. There was a big picture of a man wearing a hard hat and carrying a clipboard.

Santa turned the little wheel on the mouse and scrolled down the page. There was a series of posts. Each had a picture of Lincoln Jones: one where he was eating pizza; another where he was playing a guitar in a band; another where he was waving from the window of a big crane.

"Okay, I give up," Mrs. Claus said. "What is this?"

"Why, it's Lincoln Jones's blog," he said matter of factly.

"I can see that," she said. "But who is Lincoln Jones?"

"Oh, I forgot to mention that he is Monica's dad. You remember Monica?"

"The girl who did the nice watercolor picture of you?" Mrs. Claus asked.

"That's right," Santa said quickly. "Anyway, Monica's dad is a civil engineer. He works at big road construction sites around the U.S. Right now, he's in Michigan. Last month he was in Idaho. Since he's away from home for long periods of time, he made this blog which is just for Monica and her mom. It is private, just for the two of them."

Mrs. Claus's brows wrinkled.

Anticipating her question, Santa said, "Monica sent me the web address of her dad's blog because she wanted me to see it," Santa said pridefully, as he leaned back in the chair.

Santa continued, "Blogging was my suggestion. Her dad loves it because he gets to practice being a writer."

Santa beamed. "He tells how he's been doing, any good movies he's seen, any books he's read, some poetry he's writing, and of course how he misses them. Sometimes he puts in a little audio or video clip, so they can see him and hear him too.

Monica loves it. She sends him messages by email. And she and her mom make their own blog, so he can see what they are doing.

"A parent can maintain a good relationship with his or her child by keeping in steady contact using blogs, Skype, and emails."

Santa continued, "My favorite is email because it gives kids a chance to express themselves, and helps kids learn to think and write sentences and paragraphs."

Mrs. Claus smiled as she remembered the lines from one of Santa's poems—
"Send an email every day,
And you'll learn to write the effortless way."

"Some families have two blogs," Santa continued. "They have a special blog with email and voice or video chat just for parent and child. Then they maintain a separate social media page or blog for extended family, friends and associates.

"It is good for an away from home parent and their child to email each other at least twice every day. Some parents who are away from home set aside a special time each day when they talk to their child by telephone, or by internet phone and webcam. "

"Don't forget to tell Roland why you don't recommend social media for kids," Mrs. Claus remarked. "Or texting. "

"Thanks for reminding me," Santa exclaimed, as he grabbed his iPad to make a note to himself. "Social media is too busy and not special enough for parent and child. Texting teaches bad spelling habits and an unwholesome familiarity with strangers and gossip," Santa said a little sadly. But his eyes began to twinkle again as he took Mrs. Claus's hand, "But emails are thoughtful to compose and sweet to read.

"Children should not be surfing the internet, and they should not have a social media page or walk around texting and talking to other kids on a cell phone. Children should carry around a book to read or a ball to play with, not a mobile device.

"For kids, the cell phone or mobile device should be reserved for only conversations with parents. When a child is having some issues, and daddy is away from home, for example, it can be very comforting to have a few private moments with daddy. It is a very special moment when the phone call or email arrives that is just for her."

"Well, you better come to bed, Mr. Technology," Mrs. Claus said as she patted Santa's hand. "You have an early meeting at the toy factory, remember?"

Santa blushed. "Oh dear," he said. "You're right. I'd better go get my glass of milk and come right to bed."

Mrs. Claus shook her head and smiled as Santa headed down the stairs.

- 11 -

Santa Gets Help With His Homework

Jonathan and Kylie came bounding into Santa's office. Santa was hunched over the computer keyboard, typing away. "What are you doing, Santa?" Kylie asked.

"I'm doing my homework assignment."

"Your homework assignment?" they both exclaimed.

"Yes," said Santa. "Roland gave me a homework assignment."

"What's the assignment?" Jonathan asked.

"I've got to make two lists."

"What are the lists of?" Jonathan asked.

"Guess!" said Santa.

"Best places to buy toys online?"

"Nope."

"Bad things that kids do?"

"Nope."

"What kind of treats they should leave out for you on Christmas Eve?"

"Hmmm. No, but I like the idea," Santa said. He stroked his beard and laughed.

"We give up," they said. "What are the lists of?"

"Things I would like parents to do more of; and things I would like parents to do less of."

"You mean like more homework, discipline, taking away privileges, and grounding?"

"No," Santa said pensively. Santa sat quietly for a moment and then said, "Actually I want the list to be about patience, love, and understanding."

"Wow," Jonathan said.

"Awesome," said Kylie.

Kylie said "awesome" so seriously that Santa began to laugh. Soon he was leaning back and holding his sides. Then everyone was laughing.

Finally Santa put his arms around both Kylie and Jonathan, and giving them a big squeeze, he said, "Let's go to the kitchen and see what's in the cookie jar, and we'll continue our discussion after a little snack."

A few minutes later

"What's going on here?" Mrs. Claus asked. "You're not spoiling their appetite for dinner, are you, Mr. Claus?"

Mrs. Claus was standing in the kitchen doorway, pretending to be serious, but her smile gave her away.

Santa looked sheepish. The three were sitting at the kitchen table, the lid was off the cookie jar and there were three half empty glasses of milk on the table.

"We're helping Santa with his homework assignment."

Mrs. Claus looked puzzled.

Jonathan explained, "Santa has a homework assignment given by the guy who is writing the book on parenting. He told Santa to make two lists. Santa is doing "the more list," and we're going to do "the less list."

Mrs. Claus sat down. Santa Claus winked and said, "Maybe I better explain.

My assignment, which is due tomorrow, is to give Roland a list of things I wish parents would do more of, and a list of things I wish parents would do less of.

"The 'more' list is easy, but I got stuck on the 'less' list. Luckily, Jonathan and Kylie said that they can easily make a list of things parents should do less of."

"We're taking a little break before I get back to working on my more list. And Jonathan and Kylie are going to get started on the less list."

"I've got something for both lists," Mrs. Claus said.

"What is it?" they all asked.

"More fruit, less cookies," Mrs. Claus said.

Santa pretended he didn't hear. Kylie poked Santa in the arm.

Santa's list of things he wishes parents would do more of

Making sure kids get enough sleep (instead of letting them stay up late and making them get up early all the time).

More outdoor exercise.

More time with the family.

More fun.

More play (Santa says that for kids, playing is learning).

More reading.

Okay, kids, get ready . . . .

More work! (When Santa says "work" he means helpful chores around the house or helping others in the neighborhood or extended family). Santa says, "Real work, even if it's just sweeping a floor at grandma's or helping dad out in the yard makes you feel good when you're done."

More smiling.

More laughter.

More poetry (Santa loves poetry).

More quiet time.

More teaching and caring for kids directly instead of handing them over to strangers.

More fruit.

Jonathan and Kylie's list of things they wish parents would do less of

Less rushing around and always being in a hurry (so parents and kids will have more time to just hang out together and talk).

Less accusing us of things we didn't do and not trusting us.

Less being gone all the time.

Less making something too important and then getting upset when it doesn't work out.

Less talking about us to others (especially when it's telling them something we did wrong).

Less comparing us to others.

Less believing what someone else says about us and not believing us.

Less going out and partying with others and leaving us home with a babysitter.

Fewer vegetables. (Mrs. Claus wanted to take this out, but Santa said to leave it in because "it is Jonathan and Kylie's list and they can put in it whatever they want to.")

"Done," said Jonathan as he pushed back from the keyboard. "I've made our less list into a Word document."

Santa sat down at the keyboard, moved the mouse around and soon announced: "It's ready to print."

"High quality or low?" asked Santa.

"High," Kylie responded.

"Four copies--one for each of us and one for Roland?"

"Yes."

Santa gave a final click of the mouse and both kids waited by the printer.

"We'll give the list to Roland," Jonathan said.

- *12* -

Santa's Secret: Tender Hearted Toughness

"More salad?" Mrs. Claus asked.

"No thank you," I said.

"Have some more bread," Santa said, holding the plate up for me, while he took a piece of homemade whole wheat bread for himself.

"I'm stuffed," I said.

While I was talking to Santa, Mrs. Claus snuck a chicken drumstick onto my plate.

I laughed and said, "Okay, just one more."

"Be sure to save room for the hot apple pie," Santa said seriously.

I knew that I would somehow find room for hot apple pie.

Santa leaned back in his chair and watched me eat my drumstick. When I was about done, he said, "Well, what do you want to talk about today?"

I dabbed at my face with my napkin and said:

"When I spoke with Kylie and Jonathan and their mom, the one thing that kept coming up was how kind you and Mrs. Claus were to them.

"But being a researcher at heart, I wondered just what behaviors signify kindness to them. I figured kindness means behaviors such as hugging, giving verbal reassurances, or providing lots of good food. But like I said, these things might be what I think of as kindness, but what do they equate with kindness?

"So I asked them the open ended question: What are some of the things that Santa and Mrs. Claus do or say that are kind?

"At first I got shrugs and 'I don't know, they are just nice.' " But as the interview progressed, I just kept asking questions and listening, and before you know it, things started to come out. I took some notes, and to the best of my ability, these are some of the things they have in mind when they say that you and Mrs. Claus are kind."

I pulled some folded up papers from my pocket with scribbling on them. "I have my notes here with quotes and observations they made. Before I put them in the book, I was wondering if I could read some of them to you and see what you think."

Mrs. Claus sat down beside Santa. "Sure, go ahead," she said. Santa nodded.

I flattened out the papers, pushed my bifocals up on my nose, held the papers at arm's length, and began to read from my notes:

"Santa never yelled at us. Mrs. Claus didn't either."

Jonathan: "One time I was messing around with my trumpet while Santa was trying to talk to one of the foremen about work. He told me to wait until he was done talking, but I forgot and started playing. Santa gave me a look and said 'Knock it off!' He wasn't angry, and he wasn't yelling or anything, but he was serious. I didn't mind though, because he wasn't mean—he just said it real strong, and then he just continued talking to the foreman. Afterwards he didn't say anything. But I told him I was sorry, and he said 'No problem.'"

"Santa is like San Francisco French bread," Jonathan said. "He can be crunchy on the outside but still soft on the inside."

"The thing I liked," Kylie said, "was how Mrs. Claus discussed things with me. When she was doing some work, she would turn to me and ask 'how do you like this? Or what do you think about this?'

"She often told me things--like why she has a home office or why she got her pilot's license. It was like she was always sharing stuff. She never complained, but she told me about some hard decisions she had to make and told me what her reasoning was, and what choices she had.

"I learned so much just listening to her. I felt sometimes like I was like her friend. She didn't talk down to me, but just talked in a matter of fact way about things. She's very real."

"Yea, that's the way Santa was too," said Jonathan. "It was like he was talking out loud, thinking things through and then asking me what I thought. It got to the point that when there was an issue, I couldn't wait to hear what he was thinking.

"He never asked me any really personal stuff. Which I liked.

"The other thing I appreciated," said Jonathan, "was that he never got angry, never threw things, and he never used bad words."

Kylie agreed. She said she felt uncomfortable around angry people or people who use bad words. They both agreed that the Clauses never gossiped.

"I liked being around Santa and Mrs. Claus because there were never any put downs," Jonathan said. "And no discounting what I said. They never made fun of me or dared me to do something.

"It seems like everyone else is always teasing me about something. At school, they make fun of my clothes or because I haven't done something yet.

Jonathan continued, "Mom's better now, but she used to always snoop around and act like I did something bad when I hadn't. No one trusted me.

"But Santa trusted me," Jonathan concluded. "He let me use his computer. And once when his cell phone was missing, he didn't accuse me of taking it. It turned out that it was under one of the sofa cushions."

"Mrs. Claus always spoke highly of Santa," Kylie said. "She never said anything bad about him," Jonathan agreed. "Santa never said anything mean about Mrs. Claus either."

"I like Mrs. Claus because she was never bossy," added Kylie. "She never ordered me to do anything. She would ask me if I would mind doing this or that."

Jonathan scratched his head and said, "It's funny. The Clauses always said 'please and thank you.' Even to each other. But they never made me say please or thank you. But I think I did . . . . sometimes."

"I don't have to pretend around Santa or Mrs. Claus." Jonathan continued, "At my old school I had to pretend to be bad to fit in with the other students. In class, I had to pretend to be interested or pretend I was paying attention even when it was boring. But with Santa I don't have to pretend anything."

When I was done reading my notes, Santa and Mrs. Claus looked at each other as if they were mystified.

"We just related to them like we would anyone else," Mrs. Claus said. "We don't play favorites around here. If I have something to say, I'll say it the same way to Jonathan or Kylie as I would the elves. If there's work to be done, then I don't care who does it or who gets the credit. It's just got to be done."

"You're right," Santa added. We are polite, of course, but there's so much work to be done that we don't make a lot of small talk or beat around the bush. Getting the toys ready to deliver to the children is what we are all about here. We expect everyone to pitch in and share the load."

"Either lead, follow, or get out of the way," Mrs. Claus said and then laughed.

Memo to myself

I'm getting a little closer to understanding why the kids love Santa and Mrs. Claus so much. It seems to involve some of the following.

There was no teasing, no pressure, no bad language, and no displays of anger. Speech was polite. There was lots of talking, sharing, listening, getting opinions, and work. But always, it seems, with an elevated tone--congenial, collaborative, and never condescending.

Yet it seems that something else is going on, which must be the mysterious love I alluded to earlier. Santa and Mrs. Claus talk about not playing favorites, getting the work done, and saying what has to be said. It almost sounds impersonal or business-like. But to the kids, it felt like love! Well, all I can do is report what I found. Go and figure.

-13 -

A Happy Sad Good Bye and Santa Reads a Poem

Today was the day I would leave. All preparations had been made.

I would depart in a sleigh driven by one of Santa's assistants to an undisclosed location. There I would be met by a helicopter and taken to the transfer point. I would board a ski plane and be flown to a remote outpost. From there I would be shuttled in a four wheel drive vehicle to a private landing strip for another single engine plane ride to an unnamed town. There a chartered jet would be waiting to bring me back to a city somewhere in the U.S.

We were sitting in the living room. The fire was roaring in the fireplace. Mrs. Claus had prepared some hot apple cider and ginger bread cookies. But I wasn't hungry.

"Did you get the more and less lists okay?" Santa asked.

"Yes, I sure did. Thank you."

"We did the less list," the kids, who were sitting by the fire, said.

"Yes, I know. Thank you for that."

Everyone fell silent.

Finally, Mrs. Claus said, "Should we get someone to help carry your bags downstairs?"

"No, I'll be fine. Really," I said, trying to sound cheerful. I have to admit that I was going to miss the Clauses and Kylie and Jonathan.

They had made me feel like part of the family, and although I looked forward to getting home and starting on the book, I was frankly a bit sad to have to say goodbye.

Santa cleared his throat and spoke in a matter of fact tone. I could see that he did not want to appear sentimental.

"Send me chapters to review as soon as they are ready. If you have any questions, send me an email. I check my emails every night."

"Yes, Sir."

"We have about 10 minutes before the sleigh is ready," Santa said with a businesslike tone of voice. "I have something I would like to share."

I opened my backpack and pulled out my notepad. "I'm ready," I said, as I put on my glasses.

"Good," said Santa. He reached into the little watch pocket on his vest. He pulled out a piece of paper and began to unfold it. When he was done, he was holding an 8-1/2 by 11 piece of paper that had been folded about six times. It was well worn and wrinkled. I could see pencil writing with evidence of lots of erasing.

With eyes twinkling, Santa said, "just a little something I wrote."

"Please read it," we all said excitedly.

Kylie and Jonathan came running over and sat down cross legged on the rug, Kylie to the left of me and Jonathan to the right.

Santa began to read.

Advice from the North Pole,
by S. Claus

A little homework every day,
But be sure to give them time to play.

Puppies and playgrounds,
Crayons and story books
Checkers and marbles, pawns and rooks,
A petting zoo and a carousel turning--
Parents, please remember that playing is learning.

A little work, a little play.
Save the cleaning for a rainy day.

Dad, you are the one they look up to.
You're the coach and the captain in charge of your crew.
Honor and duty for you are a must
So they will always have someone in whom they can trust.

A little work, a little play,
A little sunshine every day.

Kids, your parents' job is not an easy one.
They have to work and can't always have fun.
They've got to provide guidance and love
They want to be soft but sometimes have to be tough.

Okay, they'll make a mistake or two
And not always say things right.
So Santa says—Kids, keep this advice in view:
Make allowances for your parents with all your might.

Don't resent your parents for any reason
Spring, summer, fall or the holiday season.
Watch out for anger, it's a terrible thing.
Let it go and you won't feel the sting.

If someone says something that isn't nice to you
You don't have to pretend you like it or agree that it's true.
Just remember not to hate and you'll be okay
Let the anger go, that's Santa's way

You'll grow big and strong and full of love.
Showered with blessings from up above.

Dad, your child looks up to you, so you mustn't fall.
Mom, you can be their teacher when your kids are small.

I visit once a year and my work is done
But you're the one who's needed every day of the year
To be with them when they're laughing and having fun
And near at hand to hug them when life brings a tear.

So take care of yourself, mom and dad.
Eat well, go for walks and get plenty of rest,
You'll see your child isn't really "bad"
Just needing extra patience when he puts you to the test.

Here's something for you to know
When I was a kid I was slow.
I couldn't do math and I wouldn't take a bath
I fidgeted, squirmed and broke my toys.
But mom, bless her heart, said "boys will be boys."

My mom never quit on me.
She had a lot of love, you see.
Nobody knows your child like you do
Calm, wise and courageous you must be
Your child is relying on you.

Limits, boundaries and a "no" they won't mind
When you are always calm, consistent and kind.
They may give you a hard time,
But your guidance is what they need.
Deep down inside they want you to succeed.

So whenever you hear the sounds of reindeer and sled
And see a sleigh's silhouette high in the moonlit night
You can snuggle and be happy in your warm and comfy bed
Remembering the words that Santa Claus said:

"May you all love each other and treat each other right
Merry Christmas, love and kisses and sleep tight."

Santa raised his eyebrows. "Well, what do you think?" he asked, as he leaned forward to hand me the paper.

"I love it, Santa," I said. "I wouldn't change a word. It will make a beautiful ending to the book."

Mrs. Claus daubed at her eyes with a handkerchief.

Jonathan, Kylie and Santa were giving each other high fives.

A worker appeared. "The sleigh is ready," he said.

We all stood up. Mrs. Claus gave me a hug and reminded me to have my gloves and scarf ready because it was chilly out. I assured her I would. Kylie and Jonathan put their coats on and stood ready to escort me to the sleigh.

Santa shook my hand, clasping it warmly with both of his. He smiled broadly. "Vaya con Dios," Santa said.

"Bless you, Santa," I said.

www.ingramcontent.com/pod-product-compliance
Lightning Source LLC
Chambersburg PA
CBHW031321040426
42443CB00005B/167